HAITI 2016 HUMAN RIGHTS REPORT

EXECUTIVE SUMMARY

Haiti is a constitutional republic with a multiparty political system. In October 2015 legislative, municipal and first-round presidential elections were held, and while there were allegations of fraud, the results conformed to international observer-estimated outcomes and were generally regarded as credible. Second-round presidential elections were postponed indefinitely in early 2016, and former president Michel Martelly left office on February 7 at the expiration of his term with no elected successor. On February 14, parliament elected Senate President Jocelerme Privert as provisional president with a 120-day mandate. On June 6, the Provisional Electoral Council (CEP) announced that it would annul the presidential results from the October 2015 election after an independent verification commission declared that it had been marred by fraud. A repeat of the first round of the presidential election took place on November 20, with a second round scheduled for January 29, 2017 if no candidate earns more than 50 percent of the votes. If a president is elected in the first round, the January 29 election will include second round races for a third of the Senate as well as local elections.

Civilian authorities maintained effective control over the security forces.

The most serious impediments to human rights involved weak democratic governance in the country worsened by the lack of an elected and functioning government; insufficient respect for the rule of law, exacerbated by a deficient judicial system; and chronic widespread corruption.

Other human rights problems included significant but isolated allegations of arbitrary and unlawful killings by government officials; allegations of use of force against suspects and protesters; severe overcrowding and poor sanitation in prisons; chronic prolonged pretrial detention; an inefficient, unreliable, and inconsistent judiciary; governmental confiscation of private property without due process. There was also rape, violence, and societal discrimination against women; child abuse; allegations of social marginalization of vulnerable populations; and trafficking in persons. Violence, including gender-based violence, and crime within the remaining internally displaced persons (IDP) camps remained a problem.

Although the government took steps to prosecute or punish government and law enforcement officials accused of committing abuses, credible reports persisted of

officials engaging in corrupt practices, and civil society groups alleged there was widespread impunity.

Section 1. Respect for the Integrity of the Person, Including Freedom from:

a. Arbitrary Deprivation of Life and other Unlawful or Politically Motivated Killings

There were isolated allegations of police and other government officials' involvement in arbitrary or unlawful killings. Some of these resulted in arrests, but there were no convictions.

On October 25, a girl was shot and killed during a fight that broke out at a post-Hurricane Matthew food distribution site in Dame-Marie. Similarly, on November 1, a boy was killed when a mob attempted to climb aboard a boat carrying supplies in Les Cayes. The Haitian National Police (HNP) Inspector General initiated an investigation into the death and administratively suspended the officer in question.

Human rights groups continued to criticize the Departmental Brigade of Operations and Interventions, a special unit of the HNP tasked with fighting crime in difficult environments.

The Office of the Inspector General (OIG) of the HNP investigated and recommended for dismissal 11 police officers implicated in homicides through October.

b. Disappearance

There were no reports of politically motivated disappearances.

In a high-profile case, after four years of legal proceedings, a court sentenced Clifford Brandt and his associate, Ricot Pierre-Val, to 18 years of penal labor for their participation in a kidnapping ring. The judge sentenced another associate, Carlo Bendel Saint-Fort, to 19 years and acquitted three other individuals accused in the case for lack of evidence.

c. Torture and Other Cruel, Inhuman, or Degrading Treatment or Punishment

The law prohibits such practices; however, there were several reports from international and domestic nongovernmental organizations (NGOs) that members of the HNP allegedly beat or otherwise abused detainees and suspects. Prisoners at times were subject to degrading treatment, in large part due to overcrowded facilities. Several reports noted corrections officers used physical punishment and psychological abuse to mistreat prisoners.

In January video circulated of two men being stripped and beaten on the floor of a police station in the Port-au-Prince suburb of Martissant. According to human rights advocates, members of the Departmental Brigade of Operations and Interventions, Departmental Unit to Maintain Order, and Corps for Intervention and Maintaining Order perpetrated the abuse. Police authorities identified five of the perpetrators, and an investigation was underway as of October.

Allegations persisted that the UN Peacekeeping and Stabilization Force (MINUSTAH) peacekeepers were involved in incidents of sexual abuse and exploitation. The United Nations reported that as of December 20, it had received four allegations during the year; two of these alleged incidents occurred during the year, one in 2015, and one for which the date of the incident was unknown.

One of the four allegations, made against a UN police officer whose nationality was unknown, involved minors. The UN investigation continued at year's end. The United Nations also investigated two other allegations, made against UN police officers from Benin and Niger. The United Nations found the allegation against the Beninese officers to be unsubstantiated; it found the allegation against the Nigerien officer to be substantiated and repatriated the officer. The fourth allegation involved military personnel from Guatemala; the Guatemalan government investigated and substantiated this allegation and penalized the officers.

These reports represented an overall decline in the number of allegations in a given year. Officials attributed the decline in part to their efforts to combat the problem, and they highlighted a zero-tolerance policy that included training, raising awareness, and enforcement.

Prison and Detention Center Conditions

Prisons and detention centers throughout the country remained overcrowded, poorly maintained, and unsanitary.

<u>Physical Conditions</u>: Prison and detention center overcrowding was severe, especially in the National Penitentiary; the Petionville women's prison; the Petit-Goave jail; and the prisons in Jeremie, Les Cayes, Port de Paix, and Hinche. The prison in Croix des Bouquets and the new prisons in Cabaret and Fort Liberte conformed to international norms and were not overcrowded. Others, including the detention facilities in Port-au-Prince, Cap Haitien, Mirabalais, Jacmel, Hinche, Les Cayes, Anse-a-Veau, and Port de Paix, exceeded the UN's prescribed capacity of 27 square feet per inmate. In some prisons detainees slept in shifts due to lack of space. Some prisons had no beds for detainees, and some cells had no access to sunlight. In others the cells often were open to the elements and lacked adequate ventilation. Many prison facilities lacked basic services such as plumbing, sanitation, waste disposal, medical services, potable water, electricity, adequate ventilation, lighting, and isolation units for contagious patients. Some prison officials used chlorine to sanitize drinking water, but in general, prisoners in older prisons did not have access to treated drinking water.

International observers indicated prisoners and detainees continued to suffer from a lack of basic hygiene, malnutrition, poor quality health care, and water-borne illness. An estimated 10 percent of the prison population suffered from malnutrition and severe anemia, while sanitation-related diseases, including scabies, diarrhea, and oral infections, were commonplace. In several prisons the Department of Corrections (DAP) and the International Committee of the Red Cross provided personal hygiene kits; in many other facilities, inmates' families provided the kits. Because of the poor security, severe understaffing, and conditions of some detention centers, some prisons did not allow prisoners out of their cells for exercise, and many prisoners spent 23 hours a day in confinement.

Many detention facilities did not contain clinics for treatment of illnesses and diseases contracted while in custody. Few prisons had the resources to treat serious medical situations. At intake, the prevalence rate of HIV among the prison population was 64 percent higher than the prevalence rate nationally. The intake prevalence rate for tuberculosis was more than 12 times higher than the national rate. The programs of several NGOs, international organizations, and donor countries, however, continued to reduce the incidence of these diseases in the prison population.

Prison conditions generally varied by inmate gender. Female inmates in coed prisons received proportionately more space in their cells than their male counterparts. Female prisoners also experienced a better quality of life than did their male counterparts due to their smaller numbers.

The DAP estimated there were 11,600 prisoners in the country's prisons as of June. In addition the DAP held some prisoners in makeshift and unofficial detention centers, such as police stations in Petit-Goave, Miragoane, Gonaives, some parts of Port-au-Prince, and other locations. Local authorities held suspects in makeshift facilities, sometimes for extended periods, without registering them with the DAP.

Corrections authorities in Port-au-Prince maintained separate penitentiaries for adult men, women, and minors. In Port-au-Prince all male prisoners under 18 years of age were to be held at the juvenile facility at Delmas 33, but due to the lack of sufficient documentation, authorities could not always verify the ages of detainees. At times authorities detained minors believed to be older, and whose ages they could not confirm, with adult inmates. Authorities moved the vast majority of these minors to juvenile detention centers within two months of verifying their ages. Outside Port-au-Prince minors and adults often occupied the same cells due to lack of available space. The new women's prison in Cabaret had the capacity to hold 300 detainees, and in October it held 254 prisoners, including 17 minors. Due to lack of space, resources, and oversight outside the capital, authorities often did not segregate juveniles from adult prisoners or convicted prisoners from pretrial detainees, as the law requires.

Prisoners' access to adequate nutrition remained a problem. The HNP has contractual and fiscal responsibility for the delivery of food to prisons. According to a UN report, changes in the contracted food suppliers and delays in fund disbursement reduced the number of meals fed to prisoners. Some prisons had kitchen facilities and employed persons to prepare and distribute food. Prison authorities generally provided prisoners with one or two meals a day, consisting of broth with flour dumplings and potatoes, rice and beans, or porridge. None of the regular meals served to prisoners provided sufficient calories, according to medical standards. Authorities allowed prisoners regular deliveries of food from relatives and friends. Human rights groups reported that families sometimes paid prison staff to deliver supplemental meals and clothing to prisoners.

The HNP also managed other service contracts at prisons, such as sewage treatment. Most prisons had insufficient sewage facilities for their populations. Since only one HNP central office handled all contracts for law enforcement and prisons, attention to sewage problems often was lacking.

<u>Administration</u>: The government did not keep adequate prison records. The effectiveness of a 2009 database created by the UN Development Program

(UNDP) and the government was limited because the UNDP system was not completely compatible with the internal recordkeeping system. Prisons utilized only handwritten paper files to document and manage inmates. There was no alternative sentencing for nonviolent offenders.

There was no prison ombudsman to handle complaints; however, the country's independent human rights monitoring body, the Office of the Citizen Protector (OPC), maintained a presence at several prison facilities and advocated for the rights and better conditions of prisoners, especially juveniles in preventive detention, and investigated credible allegations of inhuman conditions. The OPC regularly visited prisons and detention facilities in the country's 18 jurisdictions and worked closely with NGOs and civil society groups.

<u>Independent Monitoring</u>: The DAP permitted the International Committee of the Red Cross, MINUSTAH, local human rights NGOs, and other organizations to freely monitor prison conditions. These institutions and organizations investigated allegations of abuse and mistreatment of prisoners, resulting several times in the improvement of their situations.

<u>Improvements</u>: The Ministry of Justice and Public Security, with assistance from international partners, opened two new prisons that conformed to international norms. In January a new women's prison opened in Cabaret with a design capacity of 300 inmates. It is equipped with classrooms, detention cells with toilets, a health clinic, and a solar power system.

The new prison in Ft. Liberte was inaugurated in August. It had the capacity to hold 600 detainees and had its own clean drinking water supply system and a solar power system.

d. Arbitrary Arrest or Detention

The law prohibits arbitrary arrest and detention, and the constitution stipulates that authorities may arrest a person only if apprehended during the commission of a crime or based on a warrant issued by a competent official such as a justice of the peace or magistrate. Authorities must bring the detainee before a judge within 48 hours of arrest. By routinely holding prisoners in pretrial detention, authorities often failed to comply with these provisions.

The law requires that authorities refer to the HNP's OIG all cases involving allegations of police criminal misconduct. Senior police officials acknowledged receipt of several complaints alleging abuses committed by officers during the year but noted that financial, staffing, and training limitations prevented the institution from readily addressing all reports of such misconduct.

Role of the Police and Security Apparatus

The HNP is an autonomous civilian institution under the authority of a single director general and includes police, corrections, fire, emergency response, airport security, port security, and coast guard functions. HNP capabilities and professionalism continued to improve, resulting in a sustained reduction in kidnappings.

The HNP took steps toward imposing systematic discipline on officers found to have committed abuses or fraud, but civil society continued to allege widespread impunity. The HNP held monthly press conferences that served as awareness campaigns to inform the public of their roles and responsibilities and provided an opportunity to report on cases of misconduct. The OIG maintained a 24-hour hotline to receive public reports of police corruption or misconduct. As of August the OIG for the HNP had recommended 27 officers for dismissal, compared with 41 such recommendations by the OIG in 2015. The most common reasons for the recommendation of dismissal were homicide, corruption, and drug trafficking. A lack of well-trained internal investigators in the HNP slowed case investigations and impeded final resolutions.

The Ministry of Justice and Public Security, through its minister and the secretary of state for public security, provides oversight to the HNP.

The HNP Sexual and Gender-Based Violence (SGBV) unit remained underresourced and understaffed. The unit had two satellite offices at Fort National and Delmas 33. The HNP assigned officers who received SGBV training to serve as regional SGBV representatives in all 10 departments. These officers had minimal links to the SGBV unit in Port-au-Prince.

MINUSTAH has operated since 2004 with a mandate to assist and advise the government on security-related matters. As of November MINUSTAH consisted of 4,577 uniformed personnel (2,338 troops and 2,239 police). MINUSTAH retained responsibility for patrolling the remaining 31 camps for IDPs. In October the UN Security Council renewed MINUSTAH's mandate for six months at existing force levels.

Foreign governments and other entities continued to provide a wide variety of training and other types of assistance to improve police professionalism, including increasing respect for human rights. The police continued to expand its outreach to and relations with local populations in Port-au-Prince by supporting the community policing unit, which had 106 officers. The unit aimed to implement policing strategies oriented toward crime reduction and foster positive police-populace communication over aggressive interdiction.

Arrest Procedures and Treatment of Detainees

The law permits police officers to make arrests with a court-authorized warrant, or when they apprehend a suspect during the commission of a crime.

Authorities generally allowed detainees access to family members after arrest. While authorities generally acknowledged the right to counsel, most detainees could not afford a private attorney. Some departmental bar associations and legal assistance groups provided free counsel to indigents. Some NGO attorneys also provided free services to the indigent. The criminal procedure code does not allow for a functional bail system.

Arbitrary Arrest: Independent reporting confirmed instances in which, contrary to law, police without warrants or with improperly prepared warrants apprehended persons not actively committing crimes. Authorities frequently detained individuals on unspecified charges. Persons arrested reported credible instances of extortion, false charges, illegal detention, physical violence by HNP personnel, and judiciary officials' refusal to comply with basic due process requirements. The judicial system rarely observed the constitutional mandate to bring detainees before a judge within 48 hours. In some cases detainees spent years in detention without appearing before a judge.

Pretrial Detention: Prolonged pretrial detention remained a serious problem. Prison population statistics did not include the large number of persons held in police stations around the country for longer than the 48-hour maximum initial detention period. Of the approximately 11,600 prison inmates, authorities held an estimated 8,300 (or 72 percent) in pretrial detention. Approximately 71 percent of adult male prisoners and 82 percent of adult female prisoners were in pretrial detention, while 84 percent of male minors and 91 percent of female minors were pretrial detainees. Pretrial detention was significantly more prevalent in Port-au-Prince--48 percent of pretrial detainees nationally are in Port-au-Prince. As of June authorities had yet to try an estimated 88 percent of Port-au-Prince's inmates.

Many pretrial detainees had never consulted with an attorney, appeared before a judge, or been given a docket timeline. While statements from prison wardens suggested that the majority of detainees spent between two and five years in pretrial detention, reports indicated that time spent in pretrial detention was much lower and varied by geographic jurisdiction.

Between January and March, 100 percent of the 92 detainees held in the Petionville police station had surpassed the legal limit of 48 hours in detention without seeing a judge. After the government and international partners introduced a pilot program to improve procedures and oversight, that number was reduced to 7 percent between the months of March and August.

In May and June, the chief prosecutor for Port-au-Prince released 763 persons-- nearly 9 percent of the country's total pretrial detainee population.

Detainee's Ability to Challenge Lawfulness of Detention before a Court: A habeas corpus law passed in 2009 was never published by a president and therefore is not legally in effect. The OPC's national and 12 regional offices worked on behalf of citizens to verify that law enforcement and judicial authorities respected the right to due process. When authorities detained persons beyond the maximum allotted 48 hours, the OPC must intervene on their behalf to expedite the process. The OPC did not have the resources to intervene in all cases of arbitrary detention.

e. Denial of Fair Public Trial

The law provides for an independent judiciary, but senior officials in the executive and legislative branches exerted significant influence on the judicial branch and law enforcement. MINUSTAH and international and local NGOs repeatedly criticized the government for attempting to influence judicial officials. Judges assigned to politically sensitive cases complained about interference from the executive branch. With a weakened transitional government, however, local NGOs reported that influence from the executive branch decreased during the year.

Internal political divisions as well as organizational, funding, and logistical problems often hampered the efficient functioning of the Supreme Council of the Judiciary (CSPJ). The CSPJ is charged with independently overseeing judicial appointments, the discipline of judges, ethics issues, and management of the judiciary's financial resources. Half of the CSPJ membership positions were vacant as of December.

Pervasive and longstanding problems, primarily stemming from a lack of judicial oversight and professionalism, contributed to a large backlog of criminal cases. Judiciary personnel were paid haphazardly, with arrears often running into months, and worked in facilities that often lacked basic supplies. The failure to appoint or reappoint judges at the expiration of their terms further slowed the functioning of the judiciary.

The code of criminal procedure does not clearly assign criminal investigation responsibility, which it divides among police, justices of the peace, prosecutors, and investigating magistrates. As a result authorities often failed to question witnesses, complete investigations, compile complete case files, or conduct autopsies. While the law provides magistrates two months to request additional information from investigators, authorities were not supposed to invoke this delay more than twice for a given case. Magistrates often did not follow this requirement, and investigative judges frequently dropped cases or did not return them within the two-month limit. This resulted in extended pretrial detention for numerous detainees.

By law each of the country's 18 jurisdictions should twice per year convene a jury for trials involving major violent crimes. Many jurisdictions, however, convened only one jury per year because they lacked the resources to pay for them.

Corruption and a lack of judicial oversight also severely hampered the judiciary. Human rights organizations reported that several judicial officials, including judges and court clerks, arbitrarily charged fees to initiate criminal prosecutions, and that judges and prosecutors failed to respond to those who could not afford to pay. There were widespread, credible allegations of unqualified and unprofessional judges who received appointments as political favors. There were also persistent accusations that court deans, who are responsible for assigning cases to judges for investigation and review, at times assigned politically sensitive cases to judges with close ties to figures in the executive and legislative branches. Some human rights groups reported an improvement during the year due to the change in government and uncertainty and weakness in the power of the executive branch. Furthermore, the CSPJ was not effective in providing judicial accountability and transparency. Many judicial officials also held full-time occupations outside the courts, although the constitution bars judges from holding any other type of employment except teaching.

Trial Procedures

The judiciary follows a civil law system based on the Napoleonic Code that has remained largely unchanged since 1835. The constitution denies police and judicial authorities the right to interrogate suspects unless legal counsel or a representative of the suspect's choice is present or the suspect waives this right. Authorities, however, widely ignored certain constitutionally provided trial and due process rights.

The constitution provides defendants a presumption of innocence, as well as the right to attend trial, confront hostile witnesses, and call witnesses and evidence on their own behalf. Judges often denied these rights. The perception of widespread impunity also discouraged some witnesses from testifying at trials. Defendants and their attorneys had access to government-held evidence before trial, and defendants had the right of appeal. Defendants have the right to communicate with an attorney of their choice; however, legal aid programs were limited, and those who could not pay for attorneys were not always provided one free of charge. Free interpretation is not provided for defendants. As the majority of legal proceedings are conducted in French, and the most commonly spoken language is Haitian Creole, defendants were often unable to understand the proceedings.

The functioning of justice of peace courts (tribunaux de paix), the lowest courts in the judicial system, was inadequate. Judges presided in chamber based on their personal availability and often maintained separate, full-time jobs. Law enforcement personnel rarely maintained order during court proceedings, and frequently there was no court reporter. Bribes were often the principal factor in a judge's decision to hear a case.

In multiple communities, especially in rural areas, appointed communal administrators (CASECs) took the place of state judges and asserted powers of arrest, detention, and issuance of legal judgments. Some CASECs turned their offices into courtrooms. The most recent elections for CASECs took place in 2011. The next round of CASEC elections is scheduled for January 2017.

Political Prisoners and Detainees

There were no reports of political prisoners or detainees.

Civil Judicial Procedures and Remedies

Victims of alleged human rights abuses were legally able to bring their cases before a judge. Courts could award damages for human rights abuse claims brought in civil forums, but seeking such remedies was difficult and rarely successful.

Cases involving violations of an individual's human rights may be submitted through petitions by individuals or organizations to the Inter-American Commission of Human Rights, which in turn may submit the case to the Inter-American Court of Human Rights. The court can order civil remedies, including fair compensation to the individual injured.

Property Restitution

There were several highly publicized reports that the government failed to provide proportionate and timely restitution or compensation for governmental confiscation of private property.

In August a group of hooded gunmen entered an office of the Ministry of Health in Port-au-Prince on behalf of a private citizen who claimed the government seized his property illegally and demanded that the ministry returned it to him. A justice of the peace, who supported the private citizen's claim, accompanied them. Later, however, the minister of justice declared the property had been lawfully occupied after it was declared a public utility. Because of this and other recent incidents of private citizens attempting to seize property with the assistance of justices of the peace, the Ministry of Justice temporarily suspended the issuance or enforcement of any eviction orders.

f. Arbitrary or Unlawful Interference with Privacy, Family, Home, or Correspondence

The law prohibits such actions, and there were no reports that the government failed to respect these prohibitions.

Section 2. Respect for Civil Liberties, Including:

a. Freedom of Speech and Press

The law provides for freedom of speech and press, and the government generally respected these rights. The independent media were active and expressed a wide variety of views without restriction.

<u>Press and Media Freedoms</u>: There were isolated incidents of actions against journalists by national and local government officials. As a result, some independent media believed they were unable to criticize the government freely. Certain topics such as narcotics trafficking and organized crime remained largely unreported because of perceived danger.

<u>Violence and Harassment</u>: Some journalists were subjected to threats, harassment, and physical assault, allegedly due to their reporting throughout the year. In some instances government authorities participated in these acts. In January then president Martelly released a lewd song harassing journalist and human rights advocate Liliane Pierre-Paul, an outspoken critic of the Martelly administration. There was no progress in the investigation into the 2000 killing of journalist Jean Dominique or of a witness to the killing who was shot to death in March 2015.

<u>Censorship or Content Restrictions</u>: There were no reported cases of government-sponsored censorship. Human rights advocates claimed that certain government officials used public security ordinances to limit radio commentary criticizing the executive branch.

Internet Freedom

The government did not restrict or disrupt access to the internet or censor online content, and there were no credible reports that the government monitored private online communications without appropriate legal authorization. Socioeconomic and infrastructure hurdles contributed to the dominance of radio and, to a lesser extent, television, over the internet. According to the International Telecommunication Union, approximately 12 percent of citizens had access to the internet in 2015.

Academic Freedom and Cultural Events

There were no government restrictions on academic freedom or cultural events.

b. Freedom of Peaceful Assembly and Association

Freedom of Assembly

The constitution provides for freedom of assembly, and the government generally respected this right. There were several instances when police used force to impose order during demonstrations. Citizens must apply for a permit to hold legal demonstrations. Although impromptu political demonstrations in some instances provoked aggressive law enforcement responses, the police generally responded to these protests in a professional and effective manner.

Freedom of Association

The constitution provides for freedom of association, and the government generally respected this right.

c. Freedom of Religion

See the Department of State's *International Religious Freedom Report* at www.state.gov/religiousfreedomreport/.

d. Freedom of Movement, Internally Displaced Persons, Protection of Refugees, and Stateless Persons

The law provides for freedom of internal movement, foreign travel, emigration, and repatriation, and the government generally respected these rights. The government cooperated with international and humanitarian organizations, as well as other countries, in providing protection and assistance to IDPs, refugees, returning refugees, asylum seekers, stateless persons, or other persons of concern.

Foreign Travel: The Institute for Social Well-Being and Research (IBESR), under the Ministry of Social Affairs and Labor, maintained its policy of requiring minors departing the country without their parents to have parental documentation authorizing the travel. According to IBESR officials, this policy helped deter child trafficking and smuggling.

In May the chief prosecutor of Ouest Department placed overseas travel bans on nine former electoral officials and 11 cabinet ministers who had served under former president Michel Martelly, ostensibly to keep them in country to answer questions relating to corruption allegations. After a public outcry over whether the travel bans constituted political oppression and whether the prosecutor had the authority to issue the travel bans, the order was rescinded three days later.

Internally Displaced Persons

The government engaged in efforts to promote the safe, voluntary return, or resettlement of post-2010 earthquake IDPs, with substantial operational and financial support from international partners. These actions contributed to the significant decline of the earthquake-related IDP population during the year. The presence of IDP camps in the country persisted, with a large concentration of the estimated 33 remaining camps located in the greater Port-au-Prince metropolitan area. September estimates placed the number of IDPs remaining in camps at 55,107 persons or 14,593 households with 45 percent in tent or makeshift shelter sites. Statistics from the International Organization for Migration (IOM) suggested that by September, the overall post-2010 earthquake IDP population had decreased 96 percent from its estimated peak in 2010 of 1.5 million.

In the first six months of the year, the government closed four camps. Return programs carried out by the government, with the aid of international partners, accounted for all closures during this period. From these closed sites, a total of 294 households (representing 1,127 individuals) were relocated. No camps were closed through evictions.

Through the UN police force (UNPOL), MINUSTAH maintained a security presence in IDP camps and provided security in some camps with high levels of reported violence. Nonetheless, even in camps with a law enforcement presence, residents and international observers reported minimal protection from violence, including SGBV and urban crime. MINUSTAH and UNPOL members did not have arrest authority and typically functioned as a deterrent force rather than one actively engaged in law enforcement. International arrangements governing MINUSTAH's operations require a police officer to be present for any law-enforcement operation, which effectively prevented MINUSTAH officers from engaging in crime prevention in the IDP camps without a police presence. HNP understaffing sometimes prevented this partnership from functioning effectively. International workers in the camps noted that the police and MINUSTAH did not always enjoy positive relationships with IDPs. Camp residents and NGO workers reported that most police patrols, both UNPOL and HNP, monitored only the perimeter of camps and typically did not patrol after dark.

As of November the IOM's Displacement Tracking Matrix project registered approximately 14,000 people displaced by Hurricane Matthew in 61 shelters, down from an estimated immediate displacement of 175,500 people. At the surveyed sites, malaria was the most prevalent health issue, followed by influenza-like illnesses, and cholera. In coordination with the government, the United Nations developed a strategy to support the return of IDPs from collective shelters and host communities to their communities of origin. While the plan sought to ensure that the return of populations is only on a voluntary basis, IOM recorded 14 forced closures.

Protection of Refugees

Access to Asylum: The law provides for the granting of refugee status or asylum through Haitian missions or consulates abroad. Additionally, individuals could petition for asylum through the local office of the UN High Commissioner for Refugees. There were few reports, however, of requests for such status.

Stateless Persons

The dysfunctional civil registry system and weak consular capacity made obtaining documentation extremely difficult for individuals living inside or outside the country. This problem was particularly acute for many Haitians living in the Dominican Republic seeking to participate in the Dominican government's migrant regularization plan. According to the Haitian Immigrant Identification and Documentation Program, as of March fewer than 50,000 of the nearly 300,000 Haitians living in the Dominican Republic had applied for documentation through the government of Haiti's Haitian Immigrant Identification and Documentation Program, launched in 2014. Of these, only 5,000 had received passports, 38,000 had received national identity cards, and 43,000 had received birth certificates. Due to these systemic deficiencies, many Haitians living abroad were effectively stateless in their country of residence.

Section 3. Freedom to Participate in the Political Process

The law provides citizens the ability to choose their government in free and fair periodic elections held by secret ballot and based on universal and equal suffrage.

Elections and Political Participation

Recent Elections: In 2015 legislative, municipal, and first-round presidential elections were held, and while there were allegations of fraud, the results conformed to international observer estimated outcomes and were generally regarded as credible. Second-round presidential elections were postponed indefinitely in early 2016, and President Michel Martelly left office on February 7 at the end of his term with no elected successor. An accord signed on February 5 between President Martelly and the presidents of the two chambers of parliament formally agreed on a roadmap for electing a provisional president and completing 2015 elections. On February 14, parliament elected Senate President Jocelerme Privert as provisional president with a 120-day mandate. Privert established an electoral verification commission to review the October 2015 election. The commission issued its report on May 30 and recommended restarting the presidential elections due to its own conclusions that there had been irregularities, fraud, and a large number of "untraceable votes." In June the CEP accepted the recommendations and scheduled the presidential first round and select legislative races for October 9. The CEP scheduled the second round of the presidential election, select legislative races, and local elections for January 8, 2017. While Privert's 120-day mandate expired on June 14, parliament had not voted on extending his mandate as of December, but Privert nonetheless continued to function as the provisional president. On October 4, Hurricane Matthew struck southwestern Haiti causing widespread and devastating destruction, with an estimated 2.1 million people affected. Due to this natural disaster, the CEP postponed the presidential first round to November 20 and moved the second round to January 29, 2017.

November 20 elections occurred with minimal violence and disruption and with calm and orderly voting. The preliminary report by the Organization of American States Observation Mission noted significant improvements to electoral operations due to measures implemented by the electoral authorities, greater "ownership of the process" by the country, and greater civil society engagement through national observers. While voter turnout was estimated to be 21 percent, the turnout in hurricane-affected areas was higher than many expected. The CEP issued preliminary presidential results on November 28, which showed Jovenel Moise with more than 50 percent of the vote. If final results, which are scheduled to be published on January 3, 2017, determine one candidate received more than 50 percent of the vote, there will be no presidential second round.

<u>Political Parties and Political Participation</u>: The 2014 Law on Formation, Functioning, and Financing of Political Parties was not implemented. Opposition parties claimed that then president Michel Martelly improperly used government resources to support candidates from parties close to him during the August and October elections in 2015. The results of these elections were discarded but not because of government support for particular candidates.

<u>Participation of Women and Minorities</u>: No laws limit participation of women and minorities in the political process. As of December there were no female members in parliament; however, if the preliminary results from the November 20 elections

hold, there will be three female deputies (out of 119, or 2.5 percent) and one female senator (out of 30, or 3 percent). In the most recent election cycle (2015-2016), 8 percent of candidates for deputy and 10 percent of candidates for senator were women. In the period preceding the elections, female candidates expressed concerns regarding their security.

In local races the CEP enforced the constitution, which calls for "at least 30 percent women's participation in national life and in public service." As a condition to running for local races, the CEP required that each mayoral cartel (with three candidates) include one woman. All 139 mayoral cartels installed as a result of 2015 elections met this criterion. Election laws since 2008 provide significant financial incentives for political parties to field women candidates, but parties consistently failed to meet the incentive criteria. The 2015 electoral decree includes such provisions, but only 10 percent of the government's funding available for support to candidates and political parties was used for various incentives, including rewarding parties fielding higher numbers of female candidates.

Civil society actors, including unsuccessful women candidates, cited three key factors for the lack of women in politics: the lack of financing due to political parties continuing to invest more in male candidates, fear of violence and general electoral insecurity that complicates the campaigning process, and a lack of family support from parents or spouses who do not believe that a woman should be involved in politics.

As of September, three of 16 ministers and two of seven secretaries of state were women, as well as three of the nine CEP counselors, which was a slight decrease from 2015. One of the nine members of the CSPJ and one of the nine members of the country's high court were women.

Section 4. Corruption and Lack of Transparency in Government

The 2014 Law on Prevention and Repression of Corruption, the country's first anticorruption law, criminalizes a wide variety of corruption-related offenses, including illicit enrichment, bribery, embezzlement, illegal procurement, insider trading, influence peddling, and nepotism. The law imposes sentences of three to 15 years' imprisonment and gives legal authority to the government's Anticorruption Unit (ULCC) and its Financial Intelligence Unit, among others, to combat corruption.

Despite these efforts, there were numerous reports of government corruption and a perception of impunity for abusers. Law enforcement authorities and the government's anticorruption agencies launched several corruption investigations. The perception of corruption remained widespread in all branches and at all levels.

Corruption: The constitution mandates that the Senate prosecute high-level officials and parliament members accused of official corruption instead of handling such cases within the judicial system. During the year Senator Youri Latortue, chair of the Senate's Ethics and Anti-Corruption Committee, called for an investigation into the management of the PetroCaribe assistance program offered by Venezuela. The targets of Senator Latortue's investigation, including former prime ministers Jean Max Bellrive, Gary Conille, Laurent Lamothe, and Evans Paul, were all prominent officials under the two previous presidential administrations of Michel Martelly and Rene Preval. Some of the targets of Latortue's allegations decried the investigation as politically motivated, as many investigation targets were political opponents of Senator Latortue.

In another case Sandro Joseph faced corruption charges from his time as director of the National Insurance Agency from 2006 to 2008. In response Joseph issued a list of prominent citizens, including former president Rene Preval and three sitting senators, who he claimed received funds unlawfully from the agency. Joseph was acquitted of all charges in September.

There were persistent reports of corruption in the HNP. Affluent prisoners at times obtained favorable conditions of detention. The HNP investigated some allegations of police malfeasance. The OIG recommended to the Ministry of Justice that eight officers be dismissed as a result of investigations into corruption complaints, but as of October, it was unclear whether the Ministry of Justice accepted the recommendations.

A new ULCC director was appointed in April and was considered generally neutral and effective by civil society groups. Nonetheless, ULCC officials cited a lack of prosecutorial follow-through as an impediment to resolution of matters referred for prosecution.

Financial Disclosure: The law requires all senior officials of the government to file financial disclosure forms within 90 days of taking office and within 90 days of leaving office. There is no requirement for periodic reporting. Disclosure reports are confidential and not available to the public.

The sanction for failure to file financial disclosure reports is a withholding of 30 percent of the official's salary, but the government did not apply this sanction in previous years. Current government officials indicated that most officials from the departed Martelly administration were complying with those requirements.

<u>Public Access to Information</u>: No law requires the government to provide citizens access to government information.

Section 5. Governmental Attitude Regarding International and Nongovernmental Investigation of Alleged Violations of Human Rights

A number of domestic and international human rights groups generally operated without government restriction, investigating and publishing their findings on human rights cases. Government officials generally cooperated in addressing the views of various human rights groups, although they disagreed at times on the scope of certain human rights problems and the most appropriate means of addressing human rights issues.

<u>Government Human Rights Bodies</u>: The constitution provides a seven-year mandate to the OPC, the country's independent human rights ombudsperson, a post held by Florence Elie. The OPC investigated allegations of human rights abuse and worked collaboratively with international organizations. The OPC's regional representatives implemented its assistance programs throughout the country. Elie stated that despite its budget and international donor support, the institution did not possess the necessary funding or physical or human capacity to implement its strategic development and advocacy plan in each of the 10 departments. Human rights advocates and international partners noted that the OPC remained one of the country's most important national institutions responsible for independently monitoring potential human rights abuses, especially in detention centers.

In 2014 the government eliminated the position of minister delegate for human rights and the fight against extreme poverty. The minister delegate was tasked with coordinating the work of the Interministerial Human Rights Commission. Without a minister delegate to coordinate its work, the commission continued to function only on a technical level.

The Chamber of Deputies and the Senate each had a human rights committee; however, without a complete parliament, and consumed with the political crisis and lack of an elected president, the committees were largely inactive.

Section 6. Discrimination, Societal Abuses, and Trafficking in Persons

Women

<u>Rape and Domestic Violence</u>: While the law prohibits rape, it does not recognize spousal rape as a crime. The penalty for rape is a minimum of 10 years of forced labor, increasing to a mandatory 15 years if the survivor was less than 16 years old or if the rapist was a person of authority. In the case of gang rape, the maximum penalty is lifelong forced labor. Actual sentences were often less rigorous, and prosecution frequently was not pursued due to lack of reporting and follow-up on survivors' claims. The criminal code excuses a husband who kills his wife or her partner found engaging in an act of adultery in his home, but a wife who kills her husband under similar circumstances is subject to prosecution.

The law similarly does not classify domestic violence against adults as a distinct crime. Women's rights groups and human rights organizations reported that domestic violence against women remained commonplace and underreported. Police rarely arrested the perpetrators or investigated the incidents, and the survivor sometimes suffered further harassment and reprisals from perpetrators. Judges often released suspects arrested for domestic violence and rape.

SGBV was a chronic problem. International observers noted that the weakness of the justice system made it difficult for SGBV survivors to find redress, and the fear of reprisals and social stigma attached to being a survivor of SGBV contributed to underreporting and infrequent prosecutions.

Human rights groups and lawyers said barriers to reporting rape remained high and included stigmatization, fear of reprisal, and distrust of the judiciary and legal system. Multiple credible groups said that legal authorities often asked rape survivors inappropriate questions, such as whether the survivor was a virgin before the incident and what clothing the survivor was wearing at the time of the alleged rape. In some cases authorities advised survivors against pressing charges to avoid the public humiliation of a trial. Survivors of rape and other forms of sexual violence faced major obstacles in seeking legal justice, as well as access to protective services such as women's shelters.

Attorneys who represented rape survivors said that authorities were reasonably responsive to cases involving the rape of minors, as the law is clear and judicial measures exist to deal with such cases. Due to the lack of clear legal or administrative structures to deal with such cases, however, authorities frequently dropped or did not pursue cases when the offender was also a minor or the survivor was an adult.

Students at the magistrate school--who serve as judges, prosecutors, and court clerks upon graduation--received training on SGBV and strategies for improved investigation and prosecution of such crimes, victim assistance, and evidentiary procedures.

Sexual Harassment: The law does not specifically prohibit sexual harassment, although the labor code states that men and women have the same rights and obligations. Data concerning sexual harassment in the workplace were not available, but observers indicated that sexual harassment occurred, particularly in factories. Such incidents were unreported because of high unemployment and because victims had little confidence in the ability of the judicial system to provide protection.

Anecdotal evidence also suggested that sexual harassment and other derogatory treatment was a particular problem for female law enforcement officers, who constituted 9 percent of the HNP. Female police officers reported facing challenges their male counterparts did not, including less access to training, fewer promotion opportunities, and discriminatory administrative policies.

Reproductive Rights: Couples and individuals have the right to decide the number, spacing, and timing of children; manage their reproductive health; and have access to the information and means to do so, free from discrimination, coercion, and violence. Approximately 45 percent of Haitians lived in rural areas with poor access to health care services. Reports estimated the lifetime risk of maternal death to be 1 in 90, and according to UN estimates, the maternal mortality rate was 359 per 100,000 live births. According to UN Population Fund estimates, skilled health personnel attended only 37 percent of births in 2015. The primary cause of maternal death was pre-eclampsia and eclampsia (37.5 percent), followed by hemorrhage (22 percent). High maternal death rates were attributed to inadequate health-care facilities and trained health practitioners, low percentage of skilled birth attendants, and high-risk deliveries in nonqualified health facilities. Complications from abortions, which are illegal in all cases, also contributed to high maternal death rates.

Despite high levels of general knowledge of contraceptive methods and the government's active engagement, social, cultural, and legal barriers often impeded women from acquiring additional information on family planning methods and reproductive health care. In the largely conservative society, modern contraception was often socially discouraged. According to UN Population Fund 2015 estimates, only 34 percent of women ages 15-49 used a modern method of contraceptives. A lack of adequate family planning resources continued to hamper protection of women's reproductive rights. Young, sexually active women found it especially difficult to gain access to family planning services. According to a demographic survey produced by the Ministry of Public Health and Population (EMMUS 5), contraceptive prevalence among adolescent girls (ages 15-19) was only 9 percent. The adolescent birth rate remained high in 2015 at 65 per 1,000 women ages 15-19, according to UN Population Fund estimates.

Discrimination: The law does not provide for the same legal status and rights for women as for men. Women did not enjoy the same social and economic status as men, despite the constitutional amendments recognizing the principle of "at least 30 percent women's participation in national life and notably in public service."

In some social strata, tradition limited women's roles. The majority of women in rural areas remained in the traditional occupations of farming, marketing, and domestic labor. Very poor female heads of household in urban areas also often faced limited employment opportunities, working in domestic labor, sales, and as merchants.

Women continued to be underrepresented in supervisory or managerial positions in government and in the private sector. The Ministry on the Condition of Women and Women's Rights reported that while 70 percent of the government workforce consisted of women, they mostly worked in low-level positions as secretaries or janitorial staff. Conversely, women held only 12 percent of managerial positions.

By law men and women have equal protections for economic participation. In practice women faced barriers to accessing economic inputs such as land ownership; receiving profits from work (particularly agricultural labor); and securing collateral for credit, information on lending programs, and resources for financial security and growth for themselves, their families, and their businesses.

Children

Birth Registration: Citizenship is derived through an individual's parents; only one parent of either sex is necessary to transmit citizenship. Citizenship can also be acquired through a formal request to the Ministry of the Interior. The government did not register all births immediately. Birth registry is free until the age of two years, after which it can be difficult and expensive to obtain a birth certificate, particularly in the provinces. The government continued to increase efforts to reduce the number of unregistered births, particularly in the country's most impoverished rural communes.

Birth documents are legally necessary to open bank accounts, apply for credit, gain admission to hospitals, and vote. Individuals who did not possess required birth documents were not denied emergency medical services or educational opportunities on that basis.

Obtaining birth certificates was extremely difficult for individuals living outside the country (see section 2.d., Stateless Persons).

Education: Constitutional provisions require the government to provide free and compulsory primary education for all children; however, neither primary nor secondary education was compulsory, free, or universal. The government's free national education program officially continued, however, following the departure of President Martelly, the Ministry of Education shifted its focus from increasing access to education to improving the quality of education.

Child Abuse: The law prohibits domestic violence against minors. The government continued to lack sufficient resources and an adequate legal framework to fully support or enforce existing mechanisms to promote children's rights and welfare, but it made some progress in institutionalizing protections for children. The government closed several nurseries after assessing them as substandard. The government continued to station outside the capital more personnel from the Brigade for the Protection of Minors (BPM) and IBESR. The BPM and IBESR expanded partnership with international organizations and training opportunities for government officials on how better to recognize victims of child abuse and exploitation. Both offices had representatives in each of the 10 departments, as well as a presence at official border crossing points; however, most of their outreach and collaborative efforts with local community-based organizations to promote children's rights focused on Port-au-Prince.

A study launched by the Ministry of Social Affairs and Labor, published in December 2015 in collaboration with national and international organizations, estimated there were 286,000 children working in indentured domestic servitude (referred to as "restaveks"). Host families often abused restaveks and subjected them to domestic servitude, a form of trafficking in persons (see section 7.c.). The IBESR worked with international and local NGO partners to promote and strengthen community dialogue on the problems and abuses and trafficking associated with the restavek system. The IBESR initiated a national marketing campaign during the year to encourage families not to send their children away to work as domestic servants.

For more information see the Department of State's *Trafficking in Persons Report* at www.state.gov/j/tip/rls/tiprpt/ and the Department of Labor's *Findings on the Worst Forms of Child Labor* at www.dol.gov/ilab/reports/child-labor/findings/.

Port-au-Prince's population of several thousand street children, the majority of whom were boys, included not only many who were dismissed from or fled employers' homes or abusive families, including situations of domestic servitude, but also some children who lost parents or caretakers in the 2010 earthquake. NGOs reported that street children were likely to be sexually or otherwise abused, received little or no education, and were easily exploited and subjected to forced prostitution and forced begging by trafficking recruiters. Criminal gangs also reportedly forced minors to commit illegal acts. The Ministry of Social Affairs and Labor and the OPC as well as several NGOs and international organizations provided direct social support services and other assistance to street children and victims of exploitation.

The IBESR has official responsibility both for child protection and for monitoring and accrediting the country's numerous residential care centers. As of October, IBESR representatives stated there were approximately 30,000 children residing in 770 institutions nationwide. They assessed that 90 percent of residential care centers were not up to standards.

Early and Forced Marriage: The legal age of marriage is 18 years. No data was available regarding early and forced marriage, but early marriage was not a widespread custom.

Sexual Exploitation of Children: The minimum age for consensual sex is 18 years. The law prohibits the corruption of youth under the age of 21, including by prostitution, with penalties ranging from six months' to three years' imprisonment for offenders. The antitrafficking law provides significant penalties. For example, those guilty of human trafficking can serve prison sentences ranging from seven to 15 years and pay a fine ranging from HTG (Haitian Gourdes) 200,000 to HTG 1.5 million ($3,750 to $28,140), and the penalties for those guilty of human trafficking committed with aggravating circumstances is up to life imprisonment. Similar penalties apply to exploitative employers and individuals attempting to obtain sexual services from a victim of trafficking, and the law provides for increased penalties for offenders when there are aggravating circumstances, including trafficking involving minors.

Recruitment of children for sexual exploitation, pornography, and illicit activities is illegal, but the United Nations reported that armed gangs recruited children as young as 10 years old for such purposes.

<u>Displaced Children</u>: Displaced children continued to reside in IDP camps and were at risk for exploitation and abuse.

<u>Institutionalized Children</u>: Children residing in orphanages and residential care centers were at times at risk of being abused or placed in a situation of forced labor. For more information see the Department of State's *Trafficking in Persons Report* at www.state.gov/j/tip/rls/tiprpt/.

<u>International Child Abductions</u>: The country is not a party to the 1980 Hague Convention on the Civil Aspects of Child Abduction. See the Department of State's *Annual Report on International Parental Child Abduction* at travel.state.gov/content/childabduction/en/legal/compliance.html.

Anti-Semitism

The Jewish community numbered fewer than 100, and there were no reports of anti-Semitic acts.

Trafficking in Persons

See the Department of State's *Trafficking in Persons Report* at www.state.gov/j/tip/rls/tiprpt/.

Persons with Disabilities

The constitution stipulates that persons with disabilities should have the means to provide for their autonomy, education, and independence. The law prohibits discrimination in employment practices against persons with disabilities, requires the government to integrate such persons into the state's public services, and imposes a 2 percent quota for persons with disabilities in the workforces of private-sector companies. There was no information available on the extent of government enforcement of these legal protection mechanisms. Government officials also took steps to include protections for persons with disabilities to vote.

The 2010 earthquake substantially increased the size of the community of persons with disabilities. Because of widespread and chronic poverty, a shortage of public services, and limited educational opportunities, persons with disabilities remained disadvantaged. Additionally, individuals with disabilities faced significant social stigma because of their disability. Persons with mental or developmental disabilities were marginalized, neglected, and abused in society. The Office of the Secretary of State for the Integration of Handicapped Persons (BSEIPH), which falls under the Ministry of Social Affairs and Labor, is the lead government agency responsible for providing assistance to persons with disabilities and ensuring their civil, political, and social inclusion. International and local NGOs continued to provide most direct services to persons with disabilities. Access to quality medical care posed a significant challenge for persons with disabilities. Hospitals and clinics in Port-au-Prince did not have sufficient space, human resources, or public funds to treat such individuals. Where facilities existed to treat and rehabilitate them, the conditions were below international standards.

The BSEIPH has several departmental offices outside the capital and continued to refine a strategic development plan to guide the institution's efforts. The BSEIPH also offered scholarships and grants to students with disabilities and ran a program to help fund the study of disabilities-related issues at Haiti State University.

The BSEIPH ensured that existing efforts to craft or reform legislation took into account the needs of persons with disabilities. The BSEIPH provided technical assistance to governmental efforts to harmonize the labor code to the law on the integration of persons with disabilities, reform domestic adoptions framework, and conform the building code (in partnership with representatives from the Ministry of Social Affairs and Labor, IBESR, and Ministry of Public Works, Transport, and Communications) to standards of universal accessibility. Similarly, the BSEIPH worked with international NGO Handicap International and the Ministry of Public Health to develop standardized training protocols for physical therapists and other health practitioners.

In March three deaf and mute women who were travelling together, Vanesa Previl, Monique Vincent, and Jesula Gelin, were tortured and killed when they stopped at a distant relative's house to ask for shelter for the night. The relatives claimed to have believed that the women were supernatural creatures, a claim not uncommon in criminal cases in rural areas. The killings sparked large demonstrations and statements of outcry from disability rights groups, women's rights groups, and human rights groups throughout the country. A trial for those charged with the offense continued at year's end.

Acts of Violence, Discrimination, and Other Abuses Based on Sexual Orientation and Gender Identity

No laws criminalize sexual orientation or consensual same-sex conduct between adults, nor were there any reports of police officers actively perpetrating or condoning violence against members of the lesbian, gay, bisexual, transgender, and intersex (LGBTI) community.

While no laws criminalizing the changing of one's gender or sex, local attitudes remained hostile to outward LGBTI identification and expression, particularly in Port-au-Prince. Religious and other conservative organizations actively opposed the social integration of LGBTI persons and discussion of their human and civil rights. Leading presidential candidates publicly noted that they would not and should not consider any type of LGBTI rights legislation, particularly one calling for marriage equality.

No antidiscrimination laws protect LGBTI persons and minority groups. Additionally, traditional mistrust of law enforcement and judiciary officials, along with a historically low rate of successful prosecution of SGBV and related crimes, hindered LGBTI advocates and community members from successfully cooperating to reduce violence and discrimination experienced by the group. Some civil society advocates claimed that in the greater Port-au-Prince area, HNP authorities were inconsistent in their willingness to document or investigate LGBTI persons' claims of abuse.

LGBTI advocacy groups in the capital reported a greater sense of insecurity and less trust of government authorities than did groups in rural areas. Several local NGOs and international organizations provided direct support to LGBTI persons who alleged discrimination due to their sexual orientation or gender identity or being victims of SGBV.

LGBTI advocacy groups said that LGBTI individuals were uniquely targeted for abuse due to their LGBTI status. In May a gay man attended a workshop for LGBTI individuals in Gonaives. Because of his participation, his community learned that he was gay and burned down his house. In September in Pacot, just outside of Port-au-Prince, a mob burned down the home of two men suspected of being gay. A woman in Port-au-Prince was beaten by her husband when he learned she was having an affair with a woman. When she reported the crime to police officers, they refused to take her complaint allegedly because she was a lesbian. LGBTI advocacy groups said that victims were afraid to report their crimes because they were afraid of the police, and because the police themselves were afraid of repercussions from their own community if they were seen to be supporting the claims of LGBTI victims.

In September organizers of the Massimadi LGBTI film festival canceled the event due to threats of violence and a prohibition by Port au Prince chief prosecutor Danton Leger. Despite the announced cancellation of the event, the organizers of the event nonetheless received death threats and threats against the facilities hosting the festival.

Reporting of rape and sexual assault remained low across all demographics of the LGBTI community. Although advocates and international partner institutions insisted that the incidence of such abuse remained high, there was a lack of consensus among advocates on the extent of abuses. The women's victims organization KOFAVIV claimed that since the 2010 earthquake, cases of rape and other forms of SGBV perpetrated against women, children, and LGBTI persons rarely yielded arrests and convictions of the perpetrators. LGBTI advocacy groups also expressed fear of reprisal from perpetrators if they report crimes to police.

HNP academy instructors incorporated a community policing framework and philosophy, teaching police officers to respect the rights of all civilians without exception, into their human rights training curriculum. The curriculum specifically trained new officers on crimes commonly committed against the LGBTI community.

HIV and AIDS Social Stigma

In the country's most recent demographic and health survey (2012), 61 percent of women and 55 percent of men reported discriminatory attitudes towards those with HIV.

Other Societal Violence or Discrimination

According to MINUSTAH reports, vigilante reprisals, including by lynching or burning persons alive, remained a problem, especially in rural areas outside the capital. Limited or nonexistent presence of law enforcement and judicial authorities meant that in practice such reprisals had few or no legal repercussions. Citizens often retaliated against police officers, particularly after incidents in which police officers attempted to quell mob violence.

Section 7. Worker Rights

a. Freedom of Association and the Right to Collective Bargaining

Labor relations were established and regulated by a special provision of the 1984 labor code. The code provides for the right of some workers, excluding public-sector employees, to form and join unions of their choice and strike (with restrictions). The code allows for collective bargaining and requires employers to conclude a collective contract with a union if that union represents two-thirds of the workers and requests a contract. Strikes are legal provided they are approved by at least one-third of a company's workers. The code prohibits firing workers based on union activities, and employers are subject to a monetary fine for each individual violation. The code does not, however, require employers to reinstate workers illegally fired for union activity, although illegally fired workers have the right to recoup any compensation to which they are entitled.

The code places several restrictions on these rights. For instance it requires that any union obtain prior authorization from the government to be recognized. The code limits legal strikes to four types: striking while remaining at post, striking without abandoning the institution, walking out and abandoning the institution, and striking in solidarity with another strike. Public utility service workers and public-sector enterprise workers may not strike. The code defines public utility service employees as essential workers who "cannot suspend their activities without causing serious harm to public health and security." A 48-hour notice period is compulsory for all strikes, and strikes may not exceed one day. Furthermore, the law allows for compulsory arbitration at the request of only one party to halt a strike. The code does not cover freelance workers or workers in the informal economy.

The government made efforts to enforce labor laws, although its efforts were not fully effective. Government officials, unions, and factory-level affiliates also continued to expand their dialogue. Labor courts, which function under the supervision of the Ministry of Social Affairs and Labor, are responsible for adjudicating private-sector workplace conflicts. There is one labor court in Port-au-Prince. In the provinces plaintiffs had the legal option to use municipal courts for labor disputes. The code requires ministry mediation before filing cases with the labor court. In the case of a labor dispute, the ministry conducts an investigation to determine the nature and causes of the matter and facilitate a resolution. In the absence of a mutually agreed-upon resolution, the matter is referred to court.

During the year the labor ombudsperson for the textile sector and the ministry provided mediation services to workers and employers in Port-au-Prince, Caracol, and Ouanaminthe. Due to the limited capacity and procedural delays in forwarding cases from the Labor Ministry to the courts, the mediation services of the textile sector's labor ombudsperson and the conciliation services of the ministry were often the only official recourse for workers' grievances. The labor ombudsperson intervenes to improve relationships between employers, workers and trade union organizations either upon formal request by workers, unions, employers' representatives, or after observations from the International Labor Organization (ILO)'s Better Work program. The Office of the Ombudsperson uses different methods including telephone conversations, exchange meetings, factory visits and meetings, and advisory support. The labor ombudsperson helped in handling 70 cases during 2015 and had recorded 23 cases in the first nine months of 2016.

The penalty under the code for interference with union activities is 1,000 to 3,000 HTG ($19 to $57). The fines were not high enough to deter violations, and authorities did not impose or collect them. During the year the government required some factories to remedy labor violations, including violations related to freedom of association.

Antiunion discrimination persisted, although to a lesser extent than in previous years. Workers continued to report acts of suspension, termination, and other retaliation by employers on the grounds of legitimate trade union activities, membership, collective action, and other associational activity. High unemployment and antiunion sentiment among some factory workers and employers were obstacles to union organizing efforts.

There were strikes and other work stoppages in the apparel sector during the year, including disruptions in several facilities in Port-au-Prince in May as workers launched demonstrations related to pending revisions of the minimum wage. In two factories employers dismissed union members for their role in organizing these strikes. After interventions on the part of the labor ombudsperson and the ministry, the employers reinstated the workers.

The ILO and International Finance Corporation's Better Work (ILO Better Work Haiti) program noted incidences of employer interference in union activity and cases of failure to respect collective bargaining within the apparel industry.

b. Prohibition of Forced or Compulsory Labor

The law prohibits all forms of forced or compulsory labor; however, the government did not effectively enforce the law in all sectors of the economy. In the textile industry, the Labor Ministry and the labor ombudsperson made efforts to address accusations of intimidation and employer abuse and worked with factory owners to ensure that working hours complied with national labor law. The labor ombudsperson, however, did not record any instances of intimidation or employer abuse. Penalties for violations of forced labor laws range from 1,000 to 3,000 HTG ($19 to $57) but are insufficient to deter violations.

There were reports that forced or compulsory labor occurred, specifically, instances of forced labor among child domestics, or restaveks (see section 7.c.).

Also see the Department of State's *Trafficking in Persons Report* at www.state.gov/j/tip/rls/tiprpt/.

c. Prohibition of Child Labor and Minimum Age for Employment

The minimum age for employment in industrial, agricultural, or commercial companies is 15 years. The minimum age for work outside of these three sectors is 14, although children ages 12 and older may work for up to three hours per day outside of school hours in family enterprises, under Labor Ministry supervision. The law allows children age 14 to be contracted apprentices; children ages 14 to 16 may not work as apprentices more than 25 hours a week. The law prohibits young persons and children from performing any work that is likely to be hazardous; interferes with their education; or is harmful to their physical, mental, spiritual, moral, or social health and development, including the use of children in criminal activities. The law also prohibits minors from working under dangerous or hazardous conditions, such as mining, construction, or sanitation services, and it prohibits night work in industrial enterprises for minors less than 18 years of age. Prohibitions related to hazardous work, however, omit major economic sectors, including agriculture in the current assessment cycle. No textile factories were reported noncompliant with respect to child labor.

There are no legal penalties for employing children in domestic labor. The law requires employers to pay domestic workers over the age of 15 years, thereby allowing employers of domestic workers to use "food and shelter" as a means of unregulated compensation for those under 15 years of age.

Persons between the ages of 15 and 18 seeking employment must obtain a work authorization from the Labor Ministry unless they are employed in domestic service. The labor code provides for penalties for failure to follow procedures, such as obtaining work authorization to employ legally minors between the ages of 15 to 18, but it does not provide penalties for the employment of underage children. The limited penalties of between 3,000 and 5,000 HTG ($57 to $95) were not sufficient deterrents to protect children against labor exploitation.

The Labor Ministry, through the IBESR, is responsible for enforcing child labor laws. While enduring resource constraints hindered the IBESR's ability to conduct effective child labor investigations, the IBESR and the HNP's BPM responded to reports of abuse in homes and orphanages where children worked. The government does not report statistics on investigations into child labor law violations or the penalties imposed. Although the government and international donors allocated supplemental funds for the IBESR to acquire a new administrative space and hire more staff, the IBESR continued to lack sufficient social protection programs and effective legislation to eliminate the worst forms of child labor. The ministry directed law enforcement resources to rescue trafficked children working in the informal economy.

An interministerial committee that included civil society actors, unions, and employers to address the issue of child labor continued to meet throughout the year on an informal basis to discuss the challenges associated with implementing laws on child labor.

The BPM is responsible for investigating crimes against children and referred exploited and abused children to the IBESR and partner NGOs for social services. Although the BPM has the authority to respond to allegations of abuse and apprehend persons reported as exploiters of child domestic workers, the BPM did not pursue restavek cases for investigation because there were no legal penalties it could impose on those who exploited children in this manner.

Children under the age of 15 commonly worked in the informal sector to supplement family income. Activities and sectors in which children worked included domestic work, subsistence agriculture, and street trades, such as selling goods, washing cars, serving as porters in public markets and bus stations, and begging. Children also worked with parents on small family farms, although the high unemployment rate among adults kept significant numbers of children from employment on commercial farms.

The worst forms of child labor, including forced child labor, continued to be problematic and endemic--particularly in domestic service. A survey from the Labor Ministry, in partnership with national and international organizations, estimated that 286,000 children worked as restaveks in the country. Exploitation of restaveks typically included families forcing them to work excessive hours on physically demanding tasks without commensurate pay or adequate food, refusing to provide an education, and subjecting them to physical or sexual abuse. Girls were often placed in domestic servitude in private urban homes by parents who were unable to provide for them, while boys more frequently were exploited for labor on farms. Restaveks who did not run away from families usually remained with them until the age of 14. Many families forced restaveks to leave before the age of 15 to avoid paying them wages as required by law. Others ignored the law, often with impunity.

Working on the streets exposed children to a variety of hazards, including severe weather, vehicle accidents, and crime. Abandoned and runaway restaveks constituted a significant proportion of the population of children living on the street, many of whom criminal gangs exploited in prostitution or street crime, while others became street vendors or beggars.

Also see the Department of Labor's *Findings on the Worst Forms of Child Labor* at www.dol.gov/ilab/reports/child-labor/findings/.

d. Discrimination with Respect to Employment and Occupation

The constitution provides for freedom of work for all citizens and prohibits discrimination based on sex, origin, religion, opinion, or marital status. For public-sector employment, the constitution sets a minimum quota of 30 percent for women. The labor code does not define employment discrimination, although it sets out specific provisions with respect to the rights and obligations of foreigners and women such as the conditions to obtain a work permit, foreign worker quotas, and provisions related to maternity leave. The law does not prohibit discrimination based on disability, language, sexual orientation and/or gender identity, social status, or HIV-positive status.

The government took some steps to enforce the laws through administrative methods, through the Ministry of Women's Conditions and the Secretary of State for the Integration of the Disabled. In the private sector, several work areas, which had been predominantly male oriented, began engaging female workers at the same pay scale, including the public transportation and construction industries. Despite these improvements, discrimination related to gender remained a major concern, although there was no governmental assessment or report of work abuses. In the apparel sector, ILO Better Work Haiti did not issue any new findings of discrimination during the year.

e. Acceptable Conditions of Work

During the year the daily minimum wage was adjusted for all sectors, ranging from 175 HTG ($2.80) per day for domestic workers to 340 HTG ($5.44) per day in certain professions, including finance, telecommunications, and private educational institutions. In the apparel export sector, there was another increase in May, which set the minimum daily wage at 300 HTG ($4.80). The law also requires employers in the export-apparel sector to set piece rates in a manner that permits workers to earn at least 350 HTG ($5.60) for an eight-hour workday.

The law sets the standard workday for industrial, commercial, and agricultural establishments at eight hours and the workweek at 48 hours, with 24 hours of rest and paid annual holidays. It also requires payment of overtime, prohibits excessive compulsory overtime, and sets the maximum number of overtime hours allowed at 80 per trimester. The law grants exemptions to health-care, lodging, food and beverage, and entertainment establishments; managerial positions; and family establishments that employ only family members. The Labor Ministry may grant exemptions for other employers not specifically exempted by law. The law is silent with respect to prohibiting overtime for public-sector employees. The law establishes minimum health and safety regulations and requires certain provisions in regards to workers' health and safety, including quotas for onsite nurses per factory, permanent medical services, and annual medical checks. The law allows workers to notify the employer of any defect or situation that may endanger their health or safety and to call on the Labor Ministry or police if the employer fails to make the necessary ameliorations.

Although the law charges the ministry with enforcement of a range of labor-related issues, legislation on wage and hour requirements, standard workweek, premium pay for overtime, and occupational safety and health was not effectively enforced. Penalties were not sufficient to deter violations, and authorities often did not impose them. The penalty for not applying the occupational safety and health provisions of the labor code is 200 to 2,000 HTG ($3.75 to $37.50) or up to three months in prison. The penalty for violating the minimum wage or hours of work provisions of the labor code ranges from 1,000 to 3,000 HTG ($19 to $57). There were no prosecutions for the individuals accused of violating minimum wage hours of work.

The ministry's capacity to enforce the labor provisions in national and international law was limited by human resource and other constraints. Labor inspections in the capital and elsewhere faced challenges that included a lack of funding, questionable professionalism, and lack of support from law enforcement.

There were some reports of noncompliance with overtime provisions in apparel factories.

Most citizens worked in the informal sector and subsistence agriculture, for which minimum wage legislation does not apply and where daily wages of 20 to 30 HTG ($0.38 to $0.56) were common. There continued to be reports of noncompliance regarding compensation, paid leave, social security and other benefits, contracts, health services and first aid, and worker protection in the industrial and assembly sectors.

Noncompliance with safety and health standards remained a major concern. ILO Better Work Haiti continued to report that nearly all factories failed to provide the legally required number of medical facilities and staff. Other noncompliance issues included unsafe storage of chemical and hazardous materials, lack of adequate training for workers in regards to exposure to chemical and hazardous materials, and lack of protective equipment or safety warning signs.

ILO Better Work Haiti also reported cases where several workers exposed to work-related hazards failed to receive free health checks. According to the law, the annual medical exams are the responsibility of the Office of Labor Insurance, Maternity, and Accident (OFATMA). While some factories started to conduct medical checks-up independently, OFATMA began efforts to increase its capacities and also began performing medical checks at a number of factories. ILO Better Work continued to work with factories and OFATMA to improve compliance with this requirement.

No group collected formal data, but unions alleged job-related injuries occurred frequently in the construction and public-works sectors.

www.ingramcontent.com/pod-product-compliance
Lightning Source LLC
Chambersburg PA
CBHW080818280726
48660CB00018B/3513